LOOKING AFTER MY ENVIRONMENT

WITHDRAWN

Neil Morris

QEB

QEB Publishing

Published in the United States by
QEB Publishing, Inc.
3 Wrigley, Suite A
Irvine, CA 92618

www.qeb-publishing.com

Library of Congress Control Number: 2008010277

ISBN 978 1 59566 543 0

Printed and bound in United States

Author Neil Morris
Consultant Bibi van der Zee
Editor Amanda Askew
Designer Elaine Wilkinson
Picture Researcher Maria Joannou
Illustrator Mark Turner for Beehive Illustration

Publisher Steve Evans
Creative Director Zeta Davies

Words in **bold** can be found
in the glossary on page 22.

Contents

Green ideas

The **environment** is the world around us. It includes the land, air, and sea. Green ideas can help us look after our surroundings. Being "green" means caring for the environment.

You can do it

You can help the environment by starting a "Green Club." Invite your family and friends to join. Use ideas from this book and add some of your own.

You probably spend most of your time at home, in school, and around your neighborhood. This is your own special environment. It is up to you to look after it and make sure it is not spoiled.

▲ *We can all enjoy our neighborhood more if we keep it clean.*

No litterbugs!

Litter is pieces of garbage left on the ground. It spoils the environment because a lot of it is not **biodegradable**, which means that it will never rot away. You can help by making sure you are never a **litterbug**.

▲ Litterbugs make extra work for street cleaners.

Did you know?

In most countries, it is illegal to throw litter on the ground. Litterbugs can be made to pay a fine.

Litter can be as small as a candy wrapper or an old piece of chewing gum—which is very annoying when it gets stuck to your shoe! Litterbugs are thoughtless because it is easy to use a trash can, or keep things until you get home.

◄ Old chewing gum should be wrapped and put in a trash can. It is not biodegradable, so will stay on the ground forever!

Cleaning up

▲ *Some people believe that graffiti is street art, but others think it is deliberate damage.*

When spray paints are used to draw or write on walls in the street, it is called graffiti. **Local councils** usually scrub graffiti off walls, but this costs time and money.

You can do it

Ask an adult to help you to organize a litter clean-up at home or at school. You could recycle bottles, paper, and cans.

No one likes to get dog's mess on their shoes. In many countries, it is against the law to let your dog foul in a public place. Dog owners should always clean up after their dog to keep public places clean.

◄ Dog owners should be responsible and carry a bag and scoop to clean up after their dog if they need to.

Too noisy!

Near an airport or on a busy street, it is often very noisy. If the noise is too loud, it can make people unhappy because it disturbs their everyday life. This is called noise **pollution**.

Did you know?

Noise is measured in decibels. Normal conversation is about 50 decibels, loud music is about 80 decibels, and a jet engine is 120 decibels.

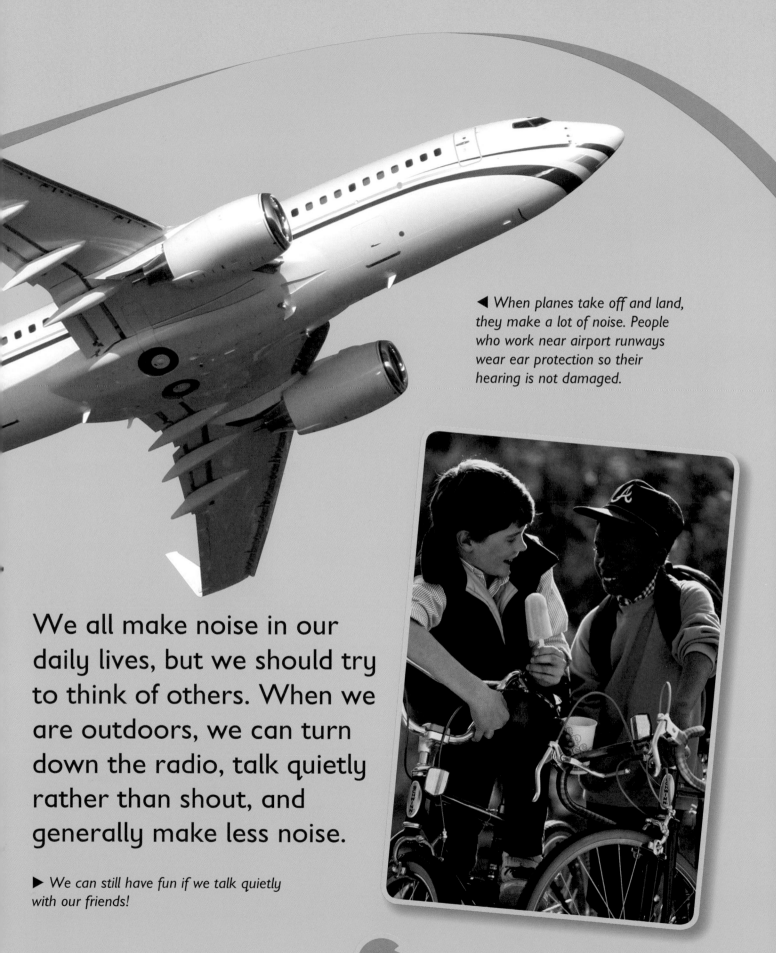

◄ When planes take off and land, they make a lot of noise. People who work near airport runways wear ear protection so their hearing is not damaged.

We all make noise in our daily lives, but we should try to think of others. When we are outdoors, we can turn down the radio, talk quietly rather than shout, and generally make less noise.

▶ We can still have fun if we talk quietly with our friends!

Fresh air

◀ We need to breathe fresh air to be healthy. There are often fewer cars in the countryside, so there is less pollution.

We breathe in oxygen gas from the air around us. All living things need this gas to live and grow. It is important that the air is clean, so we do not breathe in harmful gases.

Did you know?

The air can become dirty, even though we cannot see it. When people burn fuels to drive cars and make things in factories, waste gases are given off.

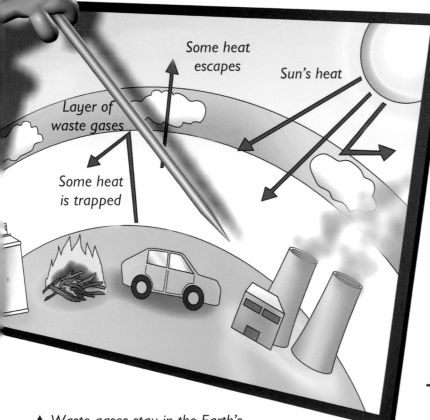

Some heat escapes

Sun's heat

Layer of waste gases

Some heat is trapped

▲ Waste gases stay in the Earth's atmosphere and stop heat from escaping. This is called the greenhouse effect.

The greenhouse effect is where waste gases act like the glass in a greenhouse. The gases can come from burning fuels, such as gasoline in a car. They trap the Sun's heat and this is slowly heating up the Earth. This process is called global warming.

Walking and cycling

We can help the environment by walking or cycling short distances, instead of riding in a car or bus. Then we will not burn fuels such as gasoline, so we do less harm to the environment.

▶ *Walking to school is fun and good for you. It also helps the environment by saving energy.*

Do you have lots of safe walking and cycling routes near your home and your school? Good sidewalks, pedestrian crossings, and cycle lanes make it easier for us to get about without polluting the air.

▲ *When you ride a bike, your muscles provide all the energy you need.*

You can do it

You and your friends could use a "walking school bus." You need an adult driver and conductor to lead you safely to school.

On vacation

◄ *A picnic is great fun. It is important not to leave any litter behind.*

On vacation, people often visit beaches and beauty spots. Picnic areas in the countryside are popular, too. These places can easily become littered because so many people visit them.

You can do it

Next time you are on the beach or having a picnic in the park, count the pieces of litter lying around. Which items make up most of the litter?

The coast and seashore are especially at risk. Big ships can pollute the shore with oil spills and the beaches become littered. In some places, **sewage** is pumped into the sea, too.

◀ *Birds' feathers can become clogged with oil from spills at sea. Wildlife protection agencies try to clean as many birds as possible.*

Tree power

Plants give off oxygen gas that we need to breathe. They also take in a gas called carbon dioxide, which we breathe out. This is why the largest plants—trees—are such an important part of the environment.

▲ Trees are important for the environment because they produce oxygen.

You can do it

Ask for permission to plant some apple and orange pips, plum stones, or conkers in your garden or school grounds. You could grow a new tree and help the environment.

The wood from trees is used to make things, including paper. We use so much wood that more trees are being cut down than are being planted. Are there plenty of trees in your local park? And are there some in your street?

▼ We need to plant more trees to replace all those that we cut down.

All together

There are lots of ways to look after our environment. We can stop littering, save energy, and use less water. We can also help to reduce pollution, keep our neighborhood clean, and recycle goods.

Did you know?

The cigarette end is the biggest litter item in the world. About 4.5 billion of them are dropped in the street every year. Next come candy wrappers and drinks cans.

▲ We can all help by taking waste to paper and bottle banks. It is much better than throwing things away.

These are green ideas, and they are all worth doing. If every one of us tries hard to do something to look after the environment, our small actions will add up to big results.

Glossary

biodegradable   something that will rot away

environment   the world around us

fuel   something that is burned to provide power

litter   small pieces of rubbish on the ground

litterbug   someone who drops things on the ground and makes litter

local council   an organization that governs, or looks after, a neighborhood, town, or district

pollution   damage to the environment caused by harmful substances

recycle   to make something new out of a thing that has been used before

sewage   liquid waste matter carried away in drains

Index

Notes for parents and teachers

- Safety. Explain the dangers of litter and waste. Children should not handle garbage directly. They should wear gloves and use litter-pickers. Children should not touch anything that they are unsure of. They must be particularly careful with glass and other sharp objects.

- Children should not challenge litterbugs. They might not take kindly to being told to pick things up and could react aggressively. As well as taking part in real clean-ups, children can play computer litter hunt games at http://news.bbc.co.uk/cbbcnews/hi/static/games/whack/cbbc_whack.stm*.

- Children must be taught not to touch excrement because of the dangers of the toxocariasis infection. This is caused by roundworm parasites found in dogs' mess. Adult dog owners should always bag their dog's waste. Use biodegradable bags and special waste containers

- If you would like more facts about noise pollution and health, visit the World Health Organization website at www.who.int/mediacentre/factsheets/fs258/en*.

- You might want to follow up the idea of a "walking school bus." Parents take it in turns to act as drivers and conductors, and follow a known route to school so that other parents can allow their children to join the "bus" along the way. There are several websites introducing the scheme, such as www.walkingbus.com*.

- The greenhouse effect and global warming are complicated issues, but are constantly in the news. There are lots of useful books and websites, including the basics of climate change at www.bbc.co.uk/climate*.

- Look through the book and talk about the pictures. Read the captions and then ask questions about other things in the photographs that have not been mentioned.

Website information is correct at time of going to press. However, the publishers cannot accept liability for any information or links found on third-party websites.